Dear Parent:

Congratulations! Your child is taking the first steps on an exciting journey. The destination? Independent reading!

STEP INTO READING® will help your child get there. The program offers five steps to reading success. Each step includes fun stories and colorful art. There are also Step into Reading Sticker Books, Step into Reading Math Readers, Step into Reading Write-In Readers, Step into Reading Phonics Readers, and Step into Reading Phonics First Steps! Boxed Sets—a complete literacy program with something for every child.

Learning to Read, Step by Step!

Ready to Read   Preschool–Kindergarten
• big type and easy words • rhyme and rhythm • picture clues
For children who know the alphabet and are eager to begin reading.

Reading with Help   Preschool–Grade 1
• basic vocabulary • short sentences • simple stories
For children who recognize familiar words and sound out new words with help.

Reading on Your Own   Grades 1–3
• engaging characters • easy-to-follow plots • popular topics
For children who are ready to read on their own.

Reading Paragraphs   Grades 2–3
• challenging vocabulary • short paragraphs • exciting stories
For newly independent readers who read simple sentences with confidence.

Ready for Chapters   Grades 2–4
• chapters • longer paragraphs • full-color art
For children who want to take the plunge into chapter books but still like colorful pictures.

STEP INTO READING® is designed to give every child a successful reading experience. The grade levels are only guides. Children can progress through the steps at their own speed, developing confidence in their reading, no matter what their grade.

Remember, a lifetime love of reading starts with a single step!

www.stepintoreading.com

Educators and librarians, for a variety of teaching tools, visit us at
www.randomhouse.com/teachers

Library of Congress Cataloging-in-Publication Data
Cobb, Annie.
Wheels! / by Annie Cobb ; illustrated by Davy Jones.
    p.   cm. — (Step into reading. A step 1 book.)
SUMMARY: Describes different kinds of wheels and what they do.
ISBN 0-679-86445-8 (trade) — ISBN 0-679-96445-2 (lib. bdg.)
1. Wheels—Juvenile literature. [1. Wheels.]
I. Jones, Davy, ill. II. Title. III. Series: Step into reading. Step 1 book.
TJ181.5 .C63 2003   621.8'11—dc21   2002013672

Printed in the United States of America   30 29 28

Wheels!

by Annie Cobb

illustrated by Davy Jones

Random House 🏠 New York

Train wheels.

Plane wheels.

Wheels in the rain.

Wheels!

Light wheels.

Bright wheels.

Wheels in the night.

Wheels!

Wide wheels.

Side wheels.

Wheels you can ride.

Wheels!

Gear wheels.

Rear wheels.

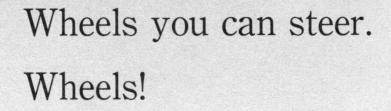

Wheels you can steer.

Wheels!

Band wheels.

Grand wheels.

Wheels in the sand.

Wheels!

Four wheels.

More wheels.

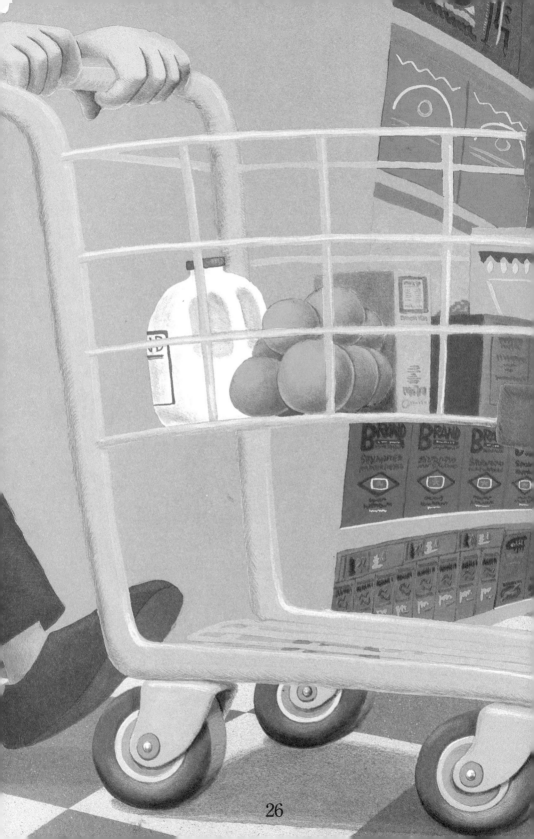

26

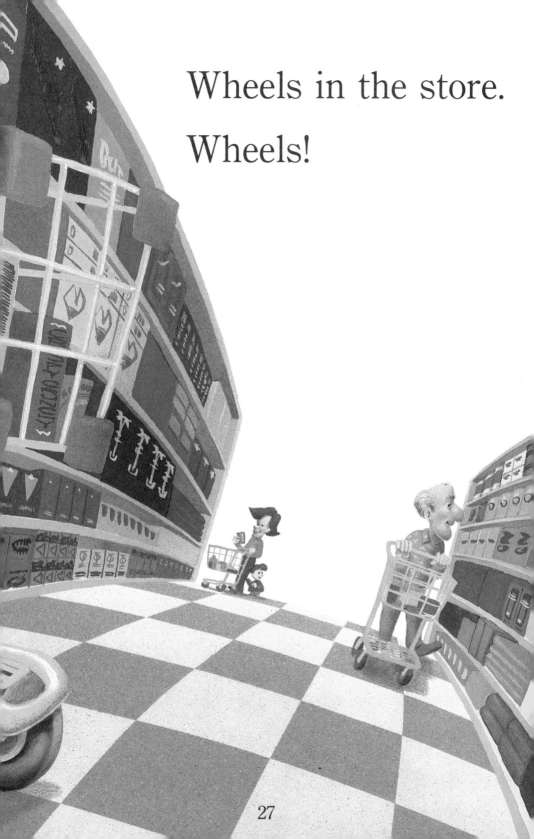

Wheels in the store.

Wheels!

Low wheels.

Tow wheels.

How would people go?

Wheels!